# CONTENTS

BARRON'S

## THE BUFFALO HUNT

Living in a dangerous
environment, the Plains Indians
survived by virtue of their
courage, daring, and skill.
Their dependence on the
buffalo was to prove their final
undoing, as the white man
sought to wipe out the Native
Americans by exterminating
the animal.

# NORTH AMERICAN
# INDIAN LIFE

BY

JOHN D. CLARE

## SIGN LANGUAGE

The Native Americans spoke many different languages. When the Europeans arrived, as many as 2,200 existed. In addition, they developed a common sign language that allowed them to communicate effectively with other tribes.

## TO DO, TO MAKE

*Place your hands together with the fingertips of your right hand touching the palm of your left. Lift both hands and shake your wrists.*

## TEPEE

*Hold knuckles lightly together, and touch the tips of your index fingers together to make the shape of a tepee.*

# Who Were the Native Americans?

### THE CAVALRY IS COMING

In the 16th century, settlers from Europe began to come to North America. In the 19th century, they began to head west. Within 50 years, Europeans had taken much of the Native Americans' land and destroyed their way of life. They believed that it had been their "manifest destiny" to do so.

**S**ince the 19th century, people have been fascinated by North American Indians. They have been portrayed in books, traveling shows, and, more recently, in films and television programs. Yet for all that, they are still misunderstood. Even the name "Indians" is misleading. Christopher Columbus called the inhabitants of the New World "Indians" because he mistakenly thought he had sailed to India. One problem is that much of what we know about the North American Indians was set down by white Americans. Some wrote to justify the slaughter and mistreatment of the native population. Another problem is that the American Indians lived and thought in a way that is alien to most of us today.

### THANKSGIVING

In 1622, the Mayflower Pilgrims, helped by the Wampanoag Indians who lived nearby, managed to bring in a good harvest. Half the Pilgrims had died in the winter of 1621, so in 1622, they joined in the tribe's annual "Thanksgiving" ceremony. The custom continued, and in 1863, Abraham Lincoln declared Thanksgiving a national holiday. In Plymouth, Massachusetts, there is a bronze statue of the Wampanoag chief, Massasoit. The inscription on the figure reads: *"Protector and Preserver of the Pilgrims."*

## NORTH AMERICAN INDIAN SETTLEMENTS

**1 ARCTIC** *Inuit.*

**2 PACIFIC NORTHWEST** *Chilkat, Coos, Kwakiutl, Tlingit, Tsimshian.*

**3 CALIFORNIA** *Yokut.*

**4 ROCKY MOUNTAINS** *Shoshoni.*

**5 GREAT PLAINS** *Arapaho, Blackfoot, Cheyenne, Crow, Mandan, Sioux.*

**6 NORTHEAST** *Algonquian, Chippewa, Huron, Midewiwin, Mohawk, Sauk.*

**7 SOUTHEAST** *Cherokee, Choctaw, Creek.*

**8 SOUTHWEST** *Apache, Zuni, Hopi, Navajo, Paiute, Pima, Pueblo.*

## THE CANYON OF THE DEAD

The Canyon de Chelly illustrates both the beauty and the history of the American West—part of the Canyon is called "Canyon del Muerto" (Spanish for "Canyon of the Dead"). This is because of a series of bloody military encounters that occurred there, and also because of the "mummy caves" in the region that hold human remains. The whole area is steeped in Native American mythology. Spider Rock, a huge pillar of rock in the Canyon more than 820 feet (250 meters) high, is the home of Spider Woman in Navajo legends (see page 18). Navajo Indians still live in the Canyon de Chelly today.

## PRE-COLUMBIAN CUP

DNA and language studies suggest that all American Indians are descended from a few families who crossed the Bering Strait in the late Ice Age. By 1492, when Columbus "discovered" America, they were living all over the continent. One particularly advanced group—the Anasazi—lived in what is now the Arizona desert. At their height, the Anasazi numbered about 5,000 people, and they accumulated huge mounds of pottery, which included cups like the one shown left.

**HORSE RIDER**

*Hold your left hand slightly downward, straight out in the "cuts paper" shape. Hold the fingers of your right hand in the "scissors"' shape, and slide onto the index finger of the left hand, as a rider would sit on a horse.*

**TRADE OR EXCHANGE**

*Make a fist with both hands, and touch the finger knuckles together. Raise both index fingers to make a "steeple."*

**YOU**

*Hold your hand in a fist and point your index finger toward the person you are referring to.*

**SETTLEMENT OR TOWN**

*A settlement is a group of people living together, so hold hands slightly downward and interlock your fingers at the ends. Point your two thumbs toward each other.*

# Wealth & Government

Today, "the American Dream" is to work hard and become wealthy, important, and famous. Many American Indians had a completely different attitude. They traded extensively, and some of them became very rich. But they refused to accumulate wealth, and acquired it mainly to give it away in shows of generosity. They thought the white Americans' habit of accumulating food and possessions was greedy and they suspected that someone who stored up wealth was a witch! Similarly, American Indians developed a way of government that was completely different from that found in European societies. Some Europeans even claimed that they had no government at all, but others conceded that—though they were impossible for white Americans to understand—American Indian ways seemed to work quite well for the American Indians.

## TOTEM POLE

The totem poles of the northwestern tribes were symbols of a family's social position and importance. This involved not only lineage (family), but also clan (a group of families) and moiety (a wide grouping of clans, linked by a common mythical ancestor). This totem pole shows a thunderbird ancestor, with other carvings symbolizing the owner's family, marriage alliances, and other important events.

## TRIBAL CHIEFS

European governments needed punishments to force their subjects to obey. American Indians cooperated voluntarily. Individuals were allowed to disagree and go their own way— even if the elders of the tribe recommended war, it was up to each warrior to decide whether or not to fight. There were few punishments—the worst punishment for an American Indian was to be banished (asked to leave the tribe).

## POTLATCH CEREMONY

This photograph shows three head men of the Chilkat tribe of the Northwest at a social event called a *potlatch*. The chiefs of the northwest coast held potlatches to demonstrate their wealth. It was obligatory to give the guests great feasts, and to load them with gifts. The most important aspect of a potlatch, however, was that guests were then obliged to hold a return potlatch, at which they had to give back twice as many presents as they had received. A potlatch, therefore, was a form of "fighting with wealth," as chiefs tried to bankrupt their rivals.

## A MANDAN CHIEF

This painting shows Four Bears, the last chief of the Mandan Indians of the Great Plains. European visitors were amazed at how little power the chiefs had. An American Indian chief could not strike the youngest warrior (even in the middle of a battle) and, at home, the only people who obeyed him were his own family. He relied on the "influence" that he had gained by his feats in battle. The feathers in Four Bears' war bonnet showed that he was a great warrior, and the knife in his headdress recalls a battle with a Cheyenne chief.

## POLE PERFECTION

The great age of totem poles came after 1850, when the American Indian carvers obtained European steel knives and chisels. Families and villages competed to commission the largest and most ornate poles—some stood 98 feet (30 meters) high. The figure on top of the totem pole on the right is a guardian spirit. On top of its hat are potlatch rings, showing that the owner of the house has held a number of successful potlatches.

# Life for Ordinary Indians

Life on the Great Plains was particularly hard, as the weather-beaten face of this old Plains Indian woman shows. One result of this was a custom known as "exposure" —sometimes, when the tribe moved on to another camp, they would leave an old person behind to starve. Old people realized that moving on might be the difference between life and death for the rest of the tribe, and often did not want to travel with their families. When the artist George Catlin spoke to one such old man, he was told: *"I am a burden to my children and I wish to die."*

**W**hen he first saw the American Indians in 1859, the prejudiced American journalist Horace Greeley decided that they belonged *"to the lowest ages of human existence—squalid and conceited, proud and worthless, lazy and lousy, they strut out their miserable existence, and at last give the world relief by dying out of it."* Conversely, present-day writers tend to depict American Indian life in an over-romanticized way. In truth, life for "ordinary" American Indians varied greatly, but most Europeans of the era would have found the Native American lifestyle uncomfortable and dangerous.

## CHOCTAW INDIAN ENCAMPMENT

Most Native American tribes were either nomadic or semi-nomadic, as in many parts of North America the weather was too unreliable to rely on farming. Many tribes spent most of the year living off the environment as hunter-gatherers. In the winter, the Choctaw Indians of the Southeast prepared the fields and planted crops such as maize, sunflowers, and sweet potatoes. In the summer, they left to go fishing and to gather fruits and berries. During this time they lived in rough temporary wooden shelters.

## STORYTELLING

When the Europeans arrived in the Americas in 1492, the American Indians had no written language. Much of their leisure time was spent listening to stories. This meant the myths and customs of the tribe were passed down from one generation to the next. Sometimes, a storyteller who was unable to walk would be carried by the young men from one village to the next, so eager were the American Indians to hear the traditional stories. In this way, elderly people played a valuable role within society.

## BEAR HUNT

American Indian bows and arrows were not powerful enough to bring down a bear, so the hunters had to kill the bear at close range. They had to go in close, then slip around under its paws and stab it in the side. Bear hunting, therefore, was very dangerous! Before they attacked the bear, American Indian hunters often prayed to the beast's spirit, asking that it give its life to benefit others.

**MAIZE BLANKET**

This woven wool Navajo blanket shows the sacred maize plant, and has a rainbow spirit surrounding it. Some American Indians believed maize had been given to them by gods called the "Corn Mothers," and attached great importance to the crop. The Hopi Indians put a maize corn doll, representing a Corn Mother, in a baby's bed for the first 20 days of its life.

# Food & Drink

**A**merican Indian women were among the first people in the world to grow plants for food, and many of the foodstuffs eaten all over the world today come from plants first domesticated in North America (including tomatoes, potatoes, and maize). The introduction of the horse by Europeans made hunting the buffalo so easy that it changed the American Indian way of life. There was less need to cultivate crops, so agriculture regressed in some areas, and tribes became dependent on the buffalo. This made it easier for the Europeans to eventually defeat them (see pages 28–29).

### HARVEST TIME

American Indians viewed farming as women's work, although children and the elderly also took part. Apache Indians of the Southwest planted small plots of land in the spring. A particularly lucky woman planted the seeds (unlucky women were never allowed to help), then tribes left their crops, living as hunter-gatherers until harvest time. In autumn, when the song of the crickets changed, the Apaches knew it was time to harvest, and they returned to their farms and brought in the crops.

### BUFFALO HUNT

By the 19th century, the buffalo hunt was at the center of Plains Indians' lives. It was the only time when strict discipline was enforced, since one wrong move could frighten away the herd. Hunting was the job of the warriors. The women and old men would drive the buffalo toward the young men, who would kill them using bows and arrows or, later, guns. The young warriors regarded it as a great honor to provide meat for the children and old people.

## FISHING

What Native Americans ate depended on where they lived. The tribespeople of California were expert fishermen, but they also killed bear. In the Rocky Mountains, the Shoshoni ate antelope and rabbits, while in the Arctic, the Inuit hunted seals and whales. In the Northeast, American Indians fished, and hunted moose and caribou.

## RESPECT FOR NATURE

The American Indians ate a great variety of foods, but they believed that they were part of nature and treated it with respect. They celebrated nature and made dining bowls in the form of animals. The Shoshoni did not kill female animals during the breeding season, and some tribes would also pray to the plant spirits as they were harvested, and would apologize if they stood on an animal by accident.

## BUFFALO

The buffalo supplied most of the wants of the Plains tribes. The tastiest cuts were eaten immediately in a great feast. The liver, tongue, and soft nose gristle were eaten raw. The knuckle-bones were chewed as we would chew gum. The rest of the meat was dried, then pounded to powder and mixed with fat to make pemmican (a small cake made of shredded meat). The hide (*parflèche*) was used for clothing, bedding, bags (see right), shields, saddles, canoes, and tepees. The hair and the sinews were used for bowstrings, rope, and thread. The horns and bones were used for arrowheads, knives, tools, dice, and cups. The hooves were used to make glue, the tail as a brush or a flyswatter, the tongue as a hair-brush, and the fat to make soap.

# Pastimes

The American Indians did not have "leisure activities" in the way that we do today, purely for enjoyment. As well as being enjoyable, their games had clear functions within their society— such as to learn important skills, to woo spirits, or to govern relations between the tribes. American Indians marked many occasions with ceremonial dances, but some also loved to race horses, gamble, play aggressive ball games with other tribes, and perform simple rhythmic music.

## PLAYING DICE

Many Native Americans loved to gamble. They believed that success in a game of chance would give them long life, wealth, children, or even good health. For the poorer members of the tribe, it was an accepted way of improving their status. Games included playing dice, playing *chungke* (a game that involved trying to throw wooden sticks into the center of a disc), and *jacksnaps* (where counters are shaken in a basket; the player with the most counters left facing upward wins).

## RATTLE AND ROLL

While the Native Americans of the Northeast played flutes, many tribes did not have instruments that could carry a tune. Instead, they accompanied their dances with drum beats, rattles, and chanting.

## PLAYING LACROSSE

American Indians invented the game of lacrosse—although it was so rough that they called it "little brother of war." Tribes would sometimes play a ball game instead of going to war with each other. Teams comprised of up to 100 players, and crowds of thousands would watch (and bet on) the result. The towns in the Creek Confederacy of tribes in the Southeast chose their alliances based on the outcome of ball games; a town defeated four times in a row by a rival town joined its side.

## MANDAN BUFFALO DANCE

Dancing was a way of communicating with the spirits. These Mandan dancers were trying to persuade the spirits to send buffalo for the hunt; their dance always worked, because it went on, day and night, until the buffalo appeared, however long it took. Dancing was central to the Native American way of life. Some tribes had "Eagle Dancers," whose swirling dance echoed the flight of the eagle, in a dance that brought peace. When it was trying to destroy American Indian culture in the 1880s, the U.S. Bureau of Indian Affairs outlawed many dance ceremonies.

## HORSE RACING

Many American Indian games were designed to improve hunting and fighting skills. Here, several Sioux warriors are taking part in a horse race. A similar game, intended to improve their horse-riding skills, involved galloping at full pace, then sliding down the side of the horse, and firing arrows underneath the neck of the horse. In another game, braves would fire arrows into the air in quick succession, competing to see who could get the most into the air at once.

# Fashion

## CHIEF KEOKUK

Keokuk was the chief of the Sauk Indians of the Northeast. In this 1834 painting by George Catlin, Keokuk is shown astride his horse, wearing battle dress and a necklace of grizzly bear claws—an emblem of real heroism. He has shaved his head, apart from a long forelock, which he has threaded through the roach headdress to attach it to his scalp. The markings on his horse were meant to bring him success in battle. In fact, despite his warlike appearance, Keokuk always advised peace. In the end, he was poisoned by his own men, who betrayed him to government agents.

During ceremonial occasions such as potlatches, many American Indians wore clothes that had deep symbolic and religious meanings. At other times, clothes were designed to demonstrate the wearer's wealth or social standing. However, there is no doubt that the American Indians thoroughly enjoyed dressing up! A warrior would wear not only tribally-produced clothing, but also items he had acquired by trade—including blankets, European suits, and even bowler hats.

## SIOUX MOCCASINS

Sioux Indians of the Plains made moccasins from two pieces of buffalo hide (a sole and an upper) that were sewn together. The Blackfoot Indians of the Plains fashioned the moccasins out of a single piece of leather, which they folded upward and sewed along the top. The shapes and colors of the beadwork were designed to bring the wearer into harmony with his environment.

## SIOUX DEERSKIN DRESS

This dress was for public or ceremonial occasions. Dresses like these were made from two deerskins—one for the front, one for the back, with an extra piece used for the yoke. In typical Sioux style, it has long fringes and tassles, and the yoke is beautifully decorated with beads. The dress was designed to show off the wealth of the family and the skill of the dressmaker, and contained symbolism that related to the individual or her family.

## ARAPAHO WAR BONNET

This is a typical Plains Indians' war bonnet. It is made from eagle feathers, tipped with horsehair and attached to a leather skullcap. The bonnet is decorated with beadwork, red tradecloth, and fur tassels. It would be worn only on important ceremonial occasions.

## BEAR-CLAW NECKLACE

This picture shows a bear-claw necklace, such as that worn by Keokuk. American Indians wore many different kinds of jewelry, including necklaces, bracelets, rings, sashes, chokers, medals, bandoliers, armbands, and breastplates. They painted their faces and bodies, and many of them were tattooed—the Pima Indians of the Southwest believed that tattoos prevented wrinkles in old age.

## ZUNI WOMAN

This Zuni woman from the Southwest is wearing a homespun woolen *manta* over a cotton blouse. American Indians made use of the materials that were commonly found in their environment. Sioux Indians used buffalo hide or deerskins, but the Paiute Indians of the Southwest used rabbit skins and the Coos Indians of the Northwest dressed their children in grasses and shredded bark. Archaeologists have even found one blanket made of 600 mouse skins.

## NATIVE AMERICAN BEADWORK SADDLEBAG

Originally, American Indian women used porcupine quills for decoration, but they started to use beads after their introduction by the Europeans. American Indian beadwork is exceptionally skillful and beautiful, as the designs on this leather saddlebag show. All the designs have a ritual symbolism.

**W**hen Europeans saw how relaxed American Indians were, they accused them of being lazy. In fact, American Indians just had different priorities than the Europeans. Their way of life was extremely rigorous, but they made sure they left time for a rich cultural life. They loved arts and crafts, and used handcrafting techniques to produce beautiful carvings, basketwork, beadwork, and clothing (see pages 12–13). However, although much of what they produced was aesthetically pleasing, it was nearly always utilitarian in nature.

## PLAINS TEPEE

The Plains Indians did not build houses; they lived in tepees, which perfectly suited their nomadic way of life. They tied together poles to make a framework, and the covering, which required the skins of up to 14 buffalo, was thrown over the framework and pegged to the ground. A hole at the top allowed smoke to escape. The American Indians covered the skins with drawings and designs, showing symbols of spiritual power they had seen in dreams or visions. The Plains Indians considered tepees the best place in the world to live. They were warm in winter, cool in summer, and were easy to move. Tepee bases also formed the shape of a circle, which was the way in which it was believed the "Power of the world" worked (see page 26).

## ZUNI POTTERY

The Plains Indians did not make pottery—it would have been far too heavy to carry around as they moved from place to place. The Pueblo Indians, however, who lived in fixed settlements, became excellent potters. They formed a flat circular base of clay, then built up the shape of the pot by layering lengths of rolled clay and smoothing the surface using a wet shell. This Zuni Indian carries a pot on her head. It is decorated with typical tri-colored geometric designs.

## PUEBLO INDIAN CLIFF PALACE

The Pueblo Indians lived in the dry, semi-desert canyons of the southwestern region. They built complicated tenements out of adobe clay bricks—the biggest apartment blocks in America until the 19th century! Pueblo houses took full advantage of solar heating. In winter, when the sun was at an angle, the adobe walls absorbed the heat, and the retained heat kept the houses warm well into the night. In summer, when the sun was overhead, its rays fell on the flat, wood roofs, which reflected the heat and kept the houses cool.

## GOING ON A BEAR HUNT

American Indian art was symbolic. When American Indian artists painted actual events, they used simple abstract drawings called pictographs, such as in this drawing of a bear hunt. They were not attempts to represent reality, but visual memory aids to remind the narrator of the details of the story. Europeans held a low opinion of American Indian art, and tried to get Native American children to draw "properly."

### SIOUX HAND DRUM

The symbolic design on this drum shows a medicine man wearing a headdress of buffalo horns. It was designed to create a spiritual link between the animal and the people who depended on it.

# Health & Medicine

## CROW MEDICINE MAN

A medicine man, such as this Crow medicine man from the Plains did much more than just heal diseases. He was the person who enlisted the support of the spirits to help the tribe, knew the drum rhythms that would attract the spirits, could lead the hunters to food, and sent magic arrows over the mountains to harm the tribe's enemies. He also gave general advice on everything from money matters to marital problems. Medicine men often became wealthy because American Indians believed that the more you paid, the harder the medicine man would try to help you.

American Indians believed that the best way to keep healthy was to live a good life in harmony with Nature—disease came when that harmony was broken. Where illness did not have an obvious cause, it was believed it may have been caused by the magic of an enemy, by a ghost, or because the patient had broken a tribal custom. The Cherokee Indians believed that disease came from the spirits of animals who sought revenge for being hunted and killed. American Indian medicine men were highly skilled at using herbal medicines and, until the middle of the 19th century, were at least as effective as European doctors. They would not have continued to hold the respect of the tribe if their cures had not worked. However, their medicine could not cure European diseases such as smallpox, and whole communities were decimated with the arrival of these virulent new illnesses.

### ROCKY MOUNTAIN IRIS

The American Indians knew thousands of herbal and plant cures. Scientists have found that many of them contain medicinal chemicals. For example, a medicine man would use white willow bark to cure a headache; today we know that it contains one of the ingredients in aspirin. The leaves of the Rocky Mountain Iris (shown in this picture) can heal septic cuts and ulcers and remove freckles. The roots, boiled and taken in small quantities, can be used to clean out and stimulate the digestive system.

## MEDICINAL ARTIFACTS

To diagnose an illness, the medicine man would first question the person to try to find out the origin of the sickness. Where this proved impossible, he would seek the help of the spirits; some sub-Arctic tribes did this by heating the shoulder blade of a moose or buffalo in the fire until it cracked and interpreted the cause from the pattern of the crack. Once the spirit causing the disease was known, the medicine man would drive it out, perhaps by frightening it away or by threatening it with a rival spirit. This illustration shows some of the instruments he might use.

## SAND PAINTING

The Navajo Indians still use sand-painting to heal the sick. Using colored sands, a healer called a *hataalii* makes the elaborate designs, which symbolically represent the stars and planets. The sick person is placed on the painting, which absorbs the negative forces causing the illness. The painting is destroyed the same day because it has fulfilled its purpose.

## ANIMAL MAGIC

This Blackfoot medicine man, painted about 1830, wears the skin of a bear, along with the skins of several snakes. It was believed wearers of skins would absorb the power and wisdom of that animal. Medicine men carried weapons to "battle" against the spirit that caused the disease.

## KWAKIUTL MARRIAGE

Here, a newly married couple from the Northwest sail back to the groom's village. Among the Kwakiutl Indians, a marriage was a way of handing down the family property to the daughter. If a man did not have a daughter, sometimes he would hold a ceremony to "marry" a part of his body (for instance his hand, or a foot) to a young man—who would thus inherit his possessions.

## EAGLE OF DELIGHT

Hayne Hudjihini, known as "Eagle of Delight," was the favorite of the five wives of Shaumonekusse, a northeastern chief who visited Washington, D.C., in 1822. In most tribes, especially those that lived on the Plains, polygamy (literally "many wives") was common. In a harsh environment, where many men died prematurely, it was a way for the tribe to provide for all the women. It was also a way for a man to show that he was rich enough to look after many wives and children. President James Monroe found Eagle of Delight pleasant and innocent. Unfortunately, she caught measles on the visit, and died soon afterward.

## SPINNING A STORY

Navajo women believed that they had been taught to weave by a spirit called Spider Woman, and they handed down both the skills and tools from mother to daughter. During the 19th century, white traders forced the weavers to use annaline chemical dyes and imported fibers, but, after 1920, the Navajo weavers returned t using vegetable dyes. Navajo women use symbols of lightning and sunbeams in the designs today as they did in the past. The early Navajo blankets were designed to be worn so their bright colors and designs could be seen "in motion."

# Love & Marriage

In American Indian society, women were responsible for the day-to-day running of the family—maintaining the tepee, planting crops and carrying out other agricultural work, collecting food and firewood, and making clothing and crafts. Occasionally, women would fight—a Crow Indian story tells how an old woman named Strikes Two drove away a party of Sioux warriors armed only with a root digger, but the men did not like to talk about it! The women also conducted trade—European traders were surprised when they found themselves doing business with women. Some historians have written that Native American women became very rich selling sex to the Europeans in exchange for casks of rum, and then selling the rum to the American Indian men.

## A DOWRY OF HORSES

In most tribes, sweethearts were allowed to meet; in others, this was forbidden, in which case the young man would have to declare his love by playing loudly on a flute. Although some marriages were arranged, most young couples married for love. When he became a warrior at about age 17, a young man would ask the girl's father for permission to marry his daughter. He would be told to provide a dowry of horses or buffalo skins. This was not a payment but a measure of how much he loved her.

## AN AMERICAN INDIAN FAMILY

Family was important to the American Indians but, in many tribes, the community was equally important. Sometimes, Inuit couples would exchange partners, and divorce was easy. On the Plains, a Cheyenne Indian simply had to throw a stick onto the ground and say *"I throw her away."* Any man who picked up the stick could become the new husband. However, the woman could take everything with her— the tepee, the tools and utensils, the fishing grounds, and the children.

# Children & Education

**A**merican Indian parents rarely punished their children, and the worst that was done to them was to ignore their demands. Native children had a strict upbringing, but they were treated with love and kindness. The whole tribe helped to bring up the children—it was not just the parents' job. The Navajo word for aunt means "little mother." Children could wander into any tent and be looked after, and it was the responsibility of the tribe to take care of orphans. At age 10, many American Indian boys went to live with, and be trained by, their uncles. A Sioux proverb runs: *"Tell me and I will listen, show me and I will understand, involve me and I will learn,"* and it was by this principle that Sioux children were educated.

## LEAVING HOME

At puberty, girls were able to marry and leave home, although Hopi girls first had to prove that they knew how to look after the household. Many tribes celebrated a girl's puberty with a ceremony or a feast. The Apache covered the girl in yellow pollen; they believed that she was especially close to the spirits during this ceremony, and that she had the power to heal the sick by touching them.

## MEDICINE BUNDLE

Between the ages of 14 and 16, a boy would undergo an initiation to become a man. The Midewiwin Indians of the eastern woodlands held an initiation ceremony at which four or five medicine men shot the boys with hallucinogenic shells. In their ensuing dreams or hallucinations, the youths would "see" a personal animal spirit friend, and were taught the secrets of adult life. When they came around, the youths would gather up a few items of religious significance to them, and keep them in a small pack called their "medicine bundle." This stayed with them for life.

## LITTLE WARRIORS

Both male and female American Indian toddlers dressed up. This little boy is wearing the war bonnet of a great warrior. American Indian children were encouraged to speak out at tribal meetings. When a boy caught his first animal, even if it was just a rabbit, a feast was held to which even the chiefs were invited. Similarly, when a girl made her first beadwork tassle, her father wore it proudly.

## SNAKE POUCH

When a baby was born in the Pima tribe, its face was painted with red ochre mixed with the mother's milk. The Pima believed that this would give the child good skin. The Sioux Indians kept the baby's umbilical cord in a specially-woven pouch. The pouch was hung from the baby's cradle in infancy, and carried by the child until puberty. The Sioux believed that this would keep the child safe.

## EARLY LEARNING

American Indian girls loved to copy their mothers, and they would look after a puppy or a doll in the same way that their mothers cared for the babies. In this way they learned the skills of motherhood.

## ON THE MOVE

Carrying a baby in a backpack left both hands free for work. Over the baby's head is a projecting hood. When the mother stopped, she could lean the cradleboard against a tree knowing that, even if it fell over facedown, the baby's head would be protected. Many American Indian mothers hung colored beads and trinkets from this hood to keep the baby amused as they walked.

# Weapons & Warfare

*T*he American Indians did not wage war for the same reasons as the white man. They did not do it to gain land, for they believed that no man could own the land, fighting instead for resources. They did not fight in armies like Europeans, and they believed that their first duty was to preserve their culture, tribal beliefs, and families. Although American Indians had fought each other for as long as Europeans had, battles were not as bloody before the arrival of the Europeans and their superior military technology.

## VALIANT WARRIORS

An American Indian fought for personal glory. Among the Plains Indians in particular, whose way of life discouraged them from gathering possessions or wealth, it was the main way to secure respect and honor from the other members of the tribe. Feathers worn by a warrior were a visual declaration of his exploits in war. A single red spot on a feather, for instance, could indicate an enemy killed in battle. Similarly, a split feather could indicate a warrior who had been wounded many times.

## COUP STICK

Because a warrior wanted honor more than anything else, he often did not kill his enemy. Much braver than killing was to ride up to a live enemy and to hit him on the chest with a stick. This was called a coup. A warrior who had "counted coup" many times was greatly honored. He was rewarded with feathers in his headdress, which could be used to display status to others.

## PIPES OF PEACE

This is a calumet—a peace pipe. A person carrying a peace pipe was safe wherever he went, and, even in the middle of a fierce battle, the warriors would stop fighting if it was held aloft.

## SCALPING

Originally, only the Mohawk Indians of the Northeast had taken scalps. As white settlers began to pay money for enemy Indian scalps (to prove that they had been killed), the practice spread to many tribes. The American Indians believed that, after death, their souls would go to the Happy Hunting Ground. There they would be pursued by their enemies—except those enemies who had been scalped. The soul of a scalped man became the possession of the victor.

## INDIAN ATTACK

American Indians waged war in a very different way from Europeans. While European armies lined up and walked into the gunfire, Indian warriors would not attack technologically superior forces head on, preferring a swift ambush. To the white soldiers, however, this seemed like cowardice and treachery. Similarly, the greatest feat for an Indian warrior was to capture an enemy's horse, and war was the means by which most tribes obtained their horses. To the Europeans, however, horse-stealing was a crime punishable by hanging.

# Transport & Technology

American Indians' attitude toward technology was different from that of the Europeans. Where the white settlers tried to tame the earth and use it to make money, American Indians saw themselves as part of nature, and survived by adapting to and cooperating with it. The Europeans regarded the American Indians as savages, and they called the eastern tribes who adopted European technology "the Civilized Tribes." But in fact, American Indian ways were not inferior to European technology and were perfectly adapted to their own environment. Indeed, the first men to go westward into the American continent ("frontiersmen" such as Davy Crockett) wore buckskin clothes and adopted American Indian technology and skills.

## SOAPSTONE PIPE

This pipe is carved from soapstone, which is soft and easy to fashion. American Indian technology was based around a series of skills—hunting, fishing, carpentry, weaving, sculpture—and their materials were all natural—skins, shells, feathers, wood, and stone. It was "craftwork" rather than technology in the modern sense.

## LONGHOUSE WALL

Static tribes used available materials to build strong, comfortable homes. The Huron Indians of the Northeast built large longhouses. They made a frame from saplings and covered it with bark and skins. Bark screens divided the interior, so each family had its own living area. This photograph shows the wall of a longhouse; it is simple but effective technology. Huron longhouses were cool in summer, warm in the cold winters, and strong enough to stand up to storms and heavy snowfalls.

## NORTHWESTERN CANOE

Canoes were built using local materials. The American Indians of the Northwest made dugout canoes like this one from the trunks of huge trees.
Craftsmen dampened the wood and used hot stones to create steam to shape the sides.
On the bows were painted pictures of moiety spirits—for instance, the killer whale, lord of the oceans.

## GUNS

Through trade, American Indians managed to get many of the white settlers' goods such as blankets, beads, metal knives, axes, and especially guns. They not only used them to make life easier, but they thought these goods had religious and magical properties—a kettle that sang was seen as being alive, and a gun that roared and killed was a *manitou* (a supernatural spirit). The Algonquian Indians of the Northeast bankrupted themselves, giving everything they had to get European trade goods to put in the graves of their dead.

## SMOKE SIGNALS

American Indians had their own unique way of communication over long distances, as effective as any European telegraph system. Messages were sent over great distances using smoke signals.

# Religion

## MORTUARY POLE

This is an eagle pole from an Indian burial place. The American Indians saw the eagle as a symbol of the power of the earth —it was graceful and beautiful, all-seeing, swift, powerful, and vicious. Most American Indian tribes buried their dead in the open, on raised wooden platforms; they believed that, as the flesh rotted, the soul was released.

*T*he first Europeans to visit North America decided that the American Indians had no religion, only superstition. In fact, the American Indians had a very sophisticated religion, which was inextricably woven into their everyday life. They prayed often and held ceremonial dances before undertaking expeditions. They divided the year into a series of Thanksgiving ceremonies, to thank the spirits for their help. American Indian religion honored the land. Native Americans believed that *"all life is holy—the two-legged sharing it with the four-legged and the wings of the air, and all green things."*

## SNOWSHOE DANCE

American Indians believed that the "Great Spirit" created the world and that the "Power of the world" worked in circles. The earth was round like a ball. The wind whirled around. Birds made their nests in circles. The seasons went around, and the life of humans was like a circle *"from childhood to childhood."* In the same way, these Mandan dancers are moving around in a circle.

## KACHINA DOLL

The Hopi Indians believed in spirits called *kachinas,* as they still do today. There are about 300 kachinas in all, although the Hopi have 30 *mong,* or chief kachinas. These spirits come from the underworld, and at one time used to live among the people, bringing them rain and good crops. But the people became disrespectful, so the kachinas left them. Now, they return during the six-month farming season, and each year kachina dancers dress up and impersonate them in a series of ceremonies.

## TAMANAWIS

Instead of a Christian God, the American Indians believed that the world contained a complex web of "powers" (or "spirits") that affected life, for better or for worse. The American Indians of the northwest coast believed in *tamanawis*—spirit-familiars in half-human, half-animal form, who could help or harm an individual, and they made masks of these spirits.

## SUN DANCE CEREMONY

Among most American Indian tribes, the main ceremony of the year was, and still is, the "Sun Dance." At the height of the ceremony, young warriors pushed skewers through their chest, and hung from them, until the flesh tore and they fell back. The Mandan Indians used the Sun Dance as a warrior's initiation ceremony—it was a way for a youth to show his courage and, through the pain, to see a vision of his "spirit-friend."

## MOUNTAIN SPIRIT DANCE

In this dance, Apache Indians called "devil dancers" dressed up as spirits. By doing so, they absorbed the powers of the spirits, and brought the tribe safety and success. Many dances were performed by "secret societies"—the American Indians believed that secrecy gave their ritual dances more power. The dance is still performed today by the tribe.

# Conflict with White Americans

## SITTING BULL

In 1868, realizing the inevitable, the Sioux agreed to move onto a large reservation in the Black Hills of Dakota. But in 1874, gold was discovered there and prospectors flooded into the area. The American government sent in the army to take the goldfields by force. The Indians fought back, led by Sitting Bull, shown here, but were defeated. In 1889, the government took still more land from the Sioux. They tried to arrest Sitting Bull, but when his family protested, the police shot him dead.

*T*he coming of the white settlers brought disaster for the American Indians. Although the American Indians won many battles, their victories provoked campaigns of mass slaughter. The American Indians were either killed or were forced to live as farmers on reservations. The Sioux chief Luther Standing Bear summed up their struggles with the white man: *"Only to the white man was Nature 'a wilderness,' and only to him was the land 'infested' with 'wild' animals and 'savage' people. To us it was tame. Not until the hairy man from the east came and with brutal frenzy heaped injustices upon our people did the 'Wild West' begin for us."*

## BUFFALO SKULLS

The white settlers wanted the American Indians' land, so they took it. In the end, they decided that extermination was the best policy. U.S. Army generals realized that on the Plains, the best way to wipe out the American Indians was to wipe out the buffalo on which they depended. *"Kill, skin and sell until the buffaloes are exterminated,"* said General Sheridan, *"then your prairies can be covered by cattle, cowboys and an advanced civilization."*

## CAPTURED BY INDIANS

*"Save the last bullet for yourself,"* was the advice given to white settlers attacked by American Indians. However, although many American Indians scalped their victims, there were very few proven examples where Indians had purposely tortured their defeated enemies.

## LITTLE BIGHORN

"Custer's Last Stand" has gone down in history as the last battle of a hero against overwhelming odds. In fact, Custer was a fool who led his 200 men into a trap. The Little Bighorn was an American Indian victory, but it was also the start of their ultimate defeat. The U.S. Army responded with a series of winter campaigns, driving the Indians from their encampments (and their food reserves). In this way, they starved the Sioux into surrender.

## GHOST DANCE

Life on the reservations was hard. Many Sioux warriors began a "ghost dance" to persuade the Great Spirit to restore the old way of things. The dancers wore ghost shirts, which they believed would protect them from the white man's bullets. Just after Christmas 1890, the army arrested a group of about 350 ghost dancers, and took them to a place called Wounded Knee. There they shot dead some 180 men, women, and children. This was the last attempt at American Indian resistance.

# Legacy of the Past

**TRADITIONAL COSTUME**

Many American Indians dress up in traditional costume on ceremonial occasions. As well as keeping a link with the past, this is also seen as a way to communicate their differences intelligibly to other Americans. This girl is attending the Red Earth Festival, one of the largest American Indian meetings.

*U*ntil the middle of the last century, the American government waged war on American Indian culture. In the 1940s, it introduced a compulsory program that sent American Indian children to boarding schools where they were not allowed to speak their native language and were taught only English-American ways. Many American Indians were damaged by the ensuing loss of identity, and the tribes still have problems with alcoholism, drug abuse, and disaffection. In 1944, however, the National Congress of American Indians was formed to reassert the American Indians' identity. Today, the American Indians form a vibrant, prosperous, and assertive community. As a modern American Indian poet writes: *"I will not allow you to ignore me. I am living. I am here."*

**EAGLE DANCER**

One way that American Indians celebrate their culture is by holding large meetings called powwows, in which they meet together to reenact the old dances and sing traditional songs.

**DIRECT ACTION**

Some American Indians are not satisfied just to celebrate native identity. They hold mass rallies and political protest meetings. In 1969, a group of activists took over Alcatraz Prison, and in 1973, some American Indians occupied the church at Wounded Knee. By protesting, they are trying to get the U.S. government to right the wrongs of the past.

## NAVAJO FAMILY

American Indian tribes now make money from tourism. The problem with this, however, is that tourism forces American Indians to act the way tourists expect them to act. They are expected to be colorful, mystical "children of nature," at peace with the environment. However, the money that tourism brings in aids new initiatives for native communities.

## THE NAVAJO NATION

Since the 1960s, the U.S. government has allowed the American Indians to run federal funding programs for their own tribal members and also to run casinos. With the money they have received, the tribes have set up businesses and health and education programs. Many American Indians today campaign for "sovereignty"—the right to govern themselves within the United States. In doing this, however, the American Indians have had to act like American businesspeople and politicians. Today, many American Indians want to "build back," and to reinstate traditional tribal structures of government.

## NAVAJO WEAVERS

In 1935 the Indian Arts and Crafts Board was set up to encourage traditional American Indian crafts. Today, there are many American Indian businesses selling "traditional" paintings, carvings, and jewelry. A skilled Navajo weaver can produce a blanket in 8 to 10 weeks, but a tapestry weaving (which has more than 30 threads to the centimeter) can take nine months. The weavers do not work from written patterns, but from traditional designs they learned as children.

# DID YOU KNOW?

That in 1821, a Cherokee Indian named Sequoyah invented a phonetic alphabet of 86 characters? This allowed him to write down the Cherokee language. By 1825, most Cherokees were literate and, in 1828, the Cherokees started publishing *The Cherokee Phoenix*, the first American Indian newspaper.

That some deities were female? The Huron Indians believed the spirit-god who created the world was female. The Hurons' battle cry was "Wiiiii"; they believed that they had been taught it by a spirit giant.

That some Indians were forbidden to speak in European courts? The state of Georgia passed a law in 1828 that forbade Indians to speak in court, even in their own defense.

That some tribes wanted to be sent to hell? When missionaries told the Huron Indians that, if they did not become Christians, they would go to hell, many Hurons said that they wanted to go to hell; they could not bear to go to heaven and leave their ancestors alone in such a terrible place.

That one white settler was made an Indian Chief? In the 1830s, a remarkable English missionary named William Duncan settled among the Tsimshian Indians of the Northwest. He started a Christian cooperative community and eventually became the chief.

That some tribes were suspicious of Christianity? When a missionary tried to convert the Iroquois Indians of the Northeast to Christianity, he was told, *"You have been preaching to the white people. We will wait a little while. If we find it makes them honest, and less disposed to cheat Indians, we will think about what you have said."*

That violence could be a way to gain social status? Among the Tlingit Indians of the Northwest, if you could not get social status by inheritance or marriage, it was regarded as quite acceptable to get it by murder!

That white Americans believed that American Indians treated their wives as slaves? That when the husband of a Chippewa Indian of the Northeast died, she had to carry a large mourning bundle for a year, during which time she could not remarry.

Picture Credits:
t=top, b=bottom, c=center, l=left, r=right, OFC=outside front cover, IFC=inside front cover, IBC=inside back cover, OBC=outside back cover

AKG (London); 4tl, 5bl, 6/7m, 16tl, 19br, 22tl, 25t, 24/25 main, 26b, 27b, 28tl. Ancient Art & Architecture; 2b, 3bl, 10bl, 27t. Ann Ronan/Image Select; 2tl. Art Resource; 6tl, 12t1,14cr. e.t.archive; IFC, 3br, 8/9t, 11t, 17b. Corbis; 29b. Gamma; 12bl, 30/31c. Hulton Getty; 5tr, 6/7t, 18/19, 21t, 28/29b. Image Select; 14br. National Geographic; 18tl. Oxford Scientific; 16bl. Photri; 7cr. SIPA Press/Rex Pictures; 30b. Spectrum; 18bl, 30t. Still Pictures; 24tl.Superstock; 3c, 4/5c, 5cr, 8bl, 10/11c, 11b, 13r, 13bl, 14b, 16/17c & 17tr, 17c, 19tr, 20tl, 21br, 22/23 main, 27cl, 28b, 29t, 31t, 31b. Werner Forman; 8tl, 9cr, 12c, 14tl, 15b, 15t, 20bl, 20/21c, 21bl, 22bl, 23tl, 23tr, 24b, 26tl.

Every effort has been made to trace the copyright holders and we apologize in advance for any unintentional omissions. We would be pleased to insert the appropriate acknowledgment in any subsequent edition of this publication.

BARRON'S

# INDEX